The Magic And The Power Of Your Subconscious Mind Made Easy

Best Way To Use Goal Setting To Get Anything You Want And How To Properly Perform Emotional Freedom Techniques Box Set

DUBL B MARKETING

THE MAGIC AND THE POWER OF YOUR SUBCONSCIOUS MIND MADE EASY

Table Of Contents

Your Free Gift

THE SCIENCE OF GETTING RICH SECRETS

GIFT: Receive a step-by-step training seminar from a top philosopher to master achieving whatever YOU WANT *FREE* ($5,000+ value)

In the guide you will learn how to master your emotions like <u>PRO's</u> and rise to the top on any and all GOALS!

Here is what is discussed...

1. The natural laws of the universe discussed in depth
2. How the natural laws can work in your favor
3. The different types of money and which kind is best to earn

As a way of saying thank you for your purchase, I'm offering a free gift that's exclusive to readers of this book.

GO TO THE LINK TO ACCESS

http://dublbmarketing.com/blog/how-to-get-anything-you-want-ebook

Best Ways To Use Goal Setting To ANYTHING You Want

Learn how by changing habits of mind can change your life!

Introduction

This is a book that will truly change one's life, if the information learned is applied. There will be a step by step process on exactly what to do for a 30-90 day period with goal setting. The information in the book was compiled by years and years of study of public figures such as Bob Proctor, Jack Canfield, Joe Vitale, Napoleon Hill, John Assaraf and etc. The book is going to focus on achieving the goal of money, but it can be applied towards achieving any goal in any area of one's life. The book will offer resources that are suggested that will help one understand the concepts better that are being discussed. The concepts that are discussed throughout this book is not theory, they are proven principles that have worked time and time again.

The entire reason for his process that will be discussed through this book is that we have to understand that our results are simply due to our thoughts. I am not going to go into great detail on the "why" our thoughts create our results, but I will offer some resources that I HIGHLY SUGGEST you check out to get a better understanding. Nevertheless, I will show you HOW to achieve your goals in anything that you want in life. You will be happy to know that you can achieve anything you want in life if you just apply the simple process that I am about to share with you.

Going back to the thoughts create results, when we take certain actions, it simply due to the fact of habits. The better word to use is PARADIGM. A paradigm is simply a multitude of habits if you can think of yourself like a thermostat. The objective of a thermostat is to keep the room at a certain temperature. If it gets too hot the AC will turn on, if it gets too cold, the AC will turn off. This is the same way a human being works. Your paradigm is your thermostat. For example, let's say you want to make $100,000.00 for the year, but you are used to making $50,000.00 in a year. You can put out maximum effort and you might even improve a little bit, but you will not achieve the $100,000.00 goal unless you change the paradigm or the setting of the thermostat.

The Importance of 30 Days Consistently

This is the chapter where I get to go over how important it is for your first 30 days of completing the system outlined in this book. The reason the first 30 days is vitally important, is because it takes about 30 days to change a habit. Early in the book I mentioned about our paradigm and how important it is to change the paradigm if we would like to change our results. In addition, I would like to say that we have many habits, so focus on changing one at a time or maybe two at most. Do not try to change more than two at a time because you will diminish your focus and this program takes some focus.

To illustrate my point about the 30 days to change a habit, I would like to support that with a study done by NASA. So a while back NASA was running test on their astronauts before they sent them in to outer space so they can test their stress levels and see how they respond or react. One of the tests is that they gave them concave glasses. This in turn caused the astronauts to see everything upside down. They were monitored every day and then on the 25th day something extraordinary happened. One of the astronauts could see everything right side up again. Then the next days following the same thing happened to the other astronauts. Now, why did this happen? Well, NASA discovered that it takes about 25-30 days for your brain to create a new neurological pathway to the new information it is processing. Now once it creates that new pathway, it restore order in your body and make what you're seeing or doing seem normal. However, NASA did another study where they put the glasses on an astronaut for 15 days and then took them off for a day and then place them back on. The result was that the astronaut still saw everything upside down and he did not see things right-side up until he had them on for about 30 days straight! I am emphasizing this story because what you are about to learn really works. There are countless stories of success, but in the beginning you must change the habit and in order to do that you have to put forth the effort for 30 days straight without any interruptions.

Step 1 – Choose a Goal

Figure out what goal or habit that you want to achieve. If you are having trouble figuring what you want, then figure out what you do not like about your life and then write down the opposite as your goal. The example that will be used throughout this book will be a goal of achieving $10,000.00 in a month through real estate.

Step 2 – Make a Goal Card and Write a Descriptive Detail of the Goal

This is where you write down exactly what you want and go into specific detail. If you do not go into detail you will attract something but it will not be exactly what you intended to attract. For example, if you want a car you want to say what the model, make, and color of the car is. Also what type of interior is in the car and all the other attributes that you would like to go with that car. You should write this down on an index card or something similar and carry it with you everywhere that you go. You want to read as many times as possible throughout the day but if nothing else, once before rising and right before you retire for the night.

You should record yourself saying this description if possible and listen to it throughout the day if you do not want to read it constantly

There is an example provided of a correct way to write your goal down and be descriptive (start everything with "I am so happy and grateful that…" and it with "…everything comes easily and effortlessly)

Example 1

I am so happy and grateful that on or before April 30, 2014 I am cheerfully making $10,000 or more in profit with the Empower Network. I am enjoying making 2 or more basic sales per day and earning $333 or more per day. I am only working 2-3 hours per day and everything comes easy and effortlessly.

Example 2

I am so happy and grateful that on or before March 30, 2014 with the power of God, I am cheerfully making $10,000 or more in profit in wholesaling real estate. I am enjoying making 2 or more real estate assignment deals per month and earning $5,000 or more each deal. I am only working 2-3 hours per day and everything comes easily and effortlessly.

Step 3 - Make a Vision Board

This is where you cut pictures out of all things that you feel relate to your goal and you make a collage or vision board
This helps your subconscious to be accustomed to seeing your goal and increases your belief that you can have you the goal

Vision Board Examples

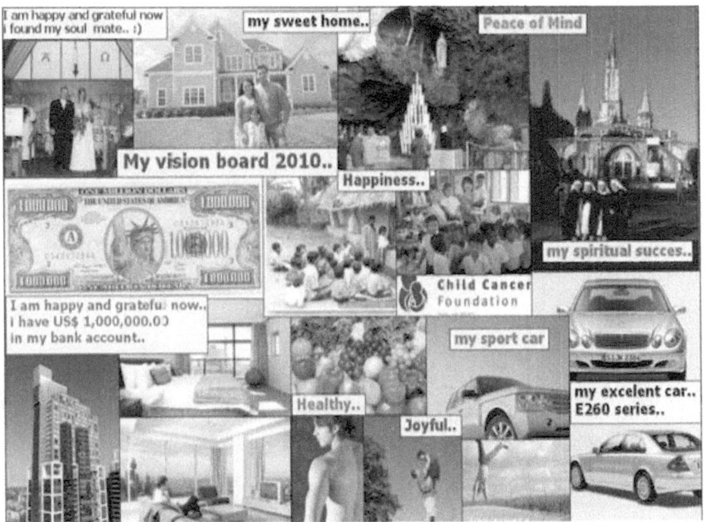

ZUMBA
Joy
Cash flow.
FUN
The Global Butterfly
Lifestyle Freedom
2010
and
2011
Playfulness
LoVe
QUEST
4CHANGE.ORG
Habitat
for Humanity
friendships inspire Spirit
triggers
MAKE-A-WISH.
A Healthy Body
Giving Back
motivate
Unstoppable
Money
JoY
Control the
"Little Voice"
in your head
Mind

A Short Message From The Author

Hey, are you enjoying the book? I'd love to hear your thoughts!

Many readers do not know how hard reviews are to come by, and how
much they help an author.

Customer Reviews

2
5.0 out of 5 stars

5 star   100%
4 star   0%
3 star   0%
2 star   0%
1 star   0%

See all verified purchase reviews ·

Share your thoughts with other customers

Write a customer review

I would be incredibly thankful if you could take just 60 seconds to write a
brief review on Amazon, even if it's just a few sentences!

>> Click here to leave a quick review

Thank you for taking the time to share your thoughts!

Your review will genuinely make a difference for me and help gain
exposure for my work.

Step 4 - Make Affirmations

Affirmations are important because it is another way to increase your belief level that you can obtain the goal. There is a correct way to write affirmations however, you want to make sure that they are positively stated and stated as if you have the goal in now. If possible you should record yourself saying the affirmation and that way you can play them while riding in your car or cleaning up the house.

You should take the affirmations that you make and apply them to a picture that represents the affirmation. This should be read upon rising every morning and before retiring and visualize yourself having the goal for a moment and then move on to the next picture and affirmation

Affirmation Examples...

I am enjoy being a professional basketball player
I am playing basketball overseas
I am enjoying being the best basketball player I am getting money like a magnet
I am living in a healthy body
I am being a great asset to my team
I am receiving many accolades for my basketball performance
I am being seen as a team player

I am enjoying being a clutch player
I am scoring the basketball at will

Examples of Affirmations and Pictures

Money Falls On
Me Like An
Avalanche

I Own A Beach House
In Southern California

My Body Is In The
Best Athletic Shape

I Have A Healthy and
Fully Functional Body

Step 5 - Create a Vision of You Already Having What You Want

This step is extremely important because the unconscious mind cannot tell if you are actually performing the task or if it is imaginary, but the same neurons and muscles will fire in your body. There was a study where doctors hooked Olympic athletes to a monitor and had them visualize themselves performing their sports. To their dismay the same muscles fired in the visualization process as when the athletes were actually performing their sport. One needs to understand that before you can achieve anything you have to see yourself achieving it and then it will come to you. So what you want to do is take out a piece of paper and write down and describe a perfect scene of you with your goal achieved.

Make sure it has sensory words that describe how it tastes, how it makes you feel, what it looks like, what the goal sounds like and how it smells. You will be visualizing what you are writing down, but you need to write down the vision so you know what to visualize.

Example: Vision Visualized For a Perfect Day

"I wake up in the morning in my bed next to my gorgeous wife who I love with all my heart and I am lucky to have. As I look to my left, I can see the sun shining through the sliding glass door that leads to the balcony that has the beach and Pacific Ocean. I go into my master bathroom to use the restroom and notice the Jack and Jill sinks, a marble counter, a Jacuzzi tub, and a shower with see through glass and a spa shower head. I come back into the room and wake my wife up to go grab some breakfast downstairs and she has on one of my dress shirts and some panties with her wild curly hair to go along with her natural beauty. When we go downstairs in our 3,000 square feet beach house we tell our cook what to fix us for breakfast and sit on a comfortable suede couch and watch sports center on a 60" flat screen LED TV that hangs on the wall. After a delicious breakfast I go throw on some gym clothes and get ready to head to the gym to play pickup basketball as me and my brother always do with current college players, pros, and ex pros. I and my wife kiss each goodbye because she is heading to the spa with her mother and sister and we head to the garage where I am hopping into our black M5 BMW, with black tail lights, black deep dish rims with a chrome lip, and a dark tint. My wife chooses to drive the black range rover rather than the Mercedes S550, or the Porsche Cayenne. I meet my brother at the gym and I am glad to see him as always and he is telling me some of his blessings as well because we are both considered successful to the world and we get our basketball run in as usual. Then we shower up at the gym and get ready to have lunch with our parents, who have spectacular health!! When eating with my parents there are a lot of laughs about the things me and Jason used to do when we were younger, but I can notice that they are stress free because they do not worry about money because Jason and I take care of all their bills and whatever money they earn, it is for them to do whatever they like. Finally, before I leave my parents and my brother, I call my wife and see if we are still on for our dinner and a movie date and she confirms with a "Yes, I can't wait!" So I tell my family goodbye with hugs and start driving back to my beach house in California. On the drive home I am just letting God know how thankful I am for my lifestyle. I don't have a stressful job or boss, I can set my own schedule, I have passive income, I am a millionaire, I and the people I love have superb health, I am constantly growing as a person, I have a financial education, I have good relationships with my wife, family and friends who I wouldn't trade in the world, and I have been blessed with finding pleasure in giving of myself and money to those that are less fortunate for whatever reason. When I get back to the house my wife is just about ready. She has a very simple outfit that is very casual to go along with her now straightened hair which is past her shoulders. So I hurry up and get ready so we can grab dinner at a Mexican restaurant that we both enjoy to eat at and be our goofy selves as we act like teenagers going out. We leave the house and this time hop in the Cayenne and enjoy our date with each other. When we come back we park the car and walk over to a beach yogurt place and grab some dessert and on the walk back, we take a stroll on the beach and notice the clear sky with all the stars and a full moon. We finally return home from a night of many giggles, smiles, and kisses and get ready to retire for the night. Me and my wife snuggle underneath the sheets in our comfortable California king bed and as I dose off I just have a feeling of joy of how lucky I am and how this has been a perfect day!!"

Step 6 - Select Meditation process

The meditation process is important and essential to achieving your goals. The reason is because you need to quiet your mind. Our mind is similar to a car engine when driving a manual shift. Often times we are driving 100mph but we are stuck in 1st gear. The meditation process allows our mind to get in the proper gear for us to visualize our goals and place it into our subconscious mind. So please don't think this is hocus pocus, but this is necessary in achieving ones goals

There are two types of meditation process that you can choose. One is to use technology and the other is to find a nice quiet place. So you decide what is more suitable for your situation.

Quiet Place

The simple and cheapest one is to find a place that you can be alone and you will not be disturbed. Turn off all cell phones while doing this because this process will allow your brain to go into a state where it can focus. Sit down and get into a comfortable position and close your eyes. Take a deep breathe in through your nose and imagine the breath of air going down into your stomach and excel the breathe out through your mouth and repeat this 6-10 times. Then just breathe in through your nose and focus on the air hitting your nostrils and excel throughout your nose. During this time your mind might wonder and that is ok, just come back and focus on the breathe of air hitting your nostrils. As you continue to do this process it will become easier for you to focus on just breathing in through your nose

Technology Method

The other meditation process would be to use *Holosync* which is a program put together to help people meditate like monks in minutes, for something that takes monks years to master. This technology does cost some money and can be found at http://www.centerpointe.com/

Daily Process to Achieve Your Goals

This process works best if you can do it for 15-30 minutes daily in the morning once waking up, but the time limit is not the most important thing because I understand that everyone has different amounts of time available with their schedules, but what is important is that you do the process daily. Now there will be days that you miss and that's fine, just pick up the process again (this applies to after the first 30 days), but the more you do the process the quicker the result will come for you. The order of the process does not matter, as long as you start with the meditation part first, because it puts your brain in a state where you can feed the information to your subconscious. If you can do the process in the same place every time it helps but it is not necessary

Step 1 - Meditate
Do whenever in the morning preferable
Do it for 15-30 minutes or whatever your schedule will allow

Step 2 - Visualize the Goal

Use the vision you created earlier in the audio and play that on the screen of your mind (5-7 minutes)

Repeat this step before you go to bed

Step 3 - Read Your Goal Card or Listen to Descriptive Detail of Your Goal

Do this step right after you get done with your visualization (read or listen to your goal a few times)

Focus on one or two goals at a time

5-7 minutes in time

Read this card all throughout the day

Make sure you read this card before you retire for the evening

Step 4 - Read or Listen to the Affirmations You Created

I recommend viewing your affirmations with the pictures of all of your goals, but if you do not want to do that, this where you can listen to your affirmations that you have created for all of your goals

You can view these throughout the day, but if nothing else once you wake up and before you retire

A Short Message From The Author

Hey! We've made it to the final chapter of the audiobook and I hope you've
enjoyed it so far.

If you have not done so yet, I would be incredibly thankful if you could take
just a minute to leave a quick review on Audible, even if it's just a sentence
or two!

Many readers and listeners don't know how hard reviews actually are to
come by, and how much they help an author.

To do so, just click the 3 dots in the top right corner of your screen inside of
your Audible app and hit the "Rate and Review" button.

Then you'll be taken to the "rate and review" page where you can enter
your star rating and then write a sentence or two.
It's that simple!

I look forward to reading your review as I personally read every single one.
I am very appreciative as your review truly makes a difference for me.

Now back to your scheduled programming.

Money Making Opportunity

I placed this chapter in the book, because often times If you would like to make more money on top of what you are already doing this is a program that I do recommend. I suggest joining the Proctor and Gallagher Institute. The reason being is that the community will allow you to become an affiliate and you can sell the products that they have in their product line, but more importantly is that they give you step by step courses and the mindset needed to succeed. This is my personal opinion, but it doesn't matter what your product/service is, but you need to have effective marketing. With this community, the education is always kept up to date because techniques in the marketing industry constantly changes. Also, the information is delivered from people who have mastered the process that is being taught. So to get more information, simply go to the link below and you can see if the community can add value to your life in some shape or form!

http://dublbmarketing.com/blog/magic-in-your-mind-review

How To Properly Perform Emotional Freedom Technique

Introduction

It works! There are certain points in our body that functions like an IPS, I mean Inter Power Supply. EFT will teach you the location of those points and how to switch them on. In this book, we will see the location of those power points and we will learn to switch them on practically.

Your Free Gift

EMOTIONAL FREEDOM TECHNIQUE

GIFT: Receive a EFT step-by-step training guide *FREE*

In the guide you will learn how to master your emotions like <u>PRO's</u> and rise to the top on any and all GOALS!

Here is what is discussed...

1. The statements to say while tapping.
2. The locations of the places on the body to tap
3. How often and when to tap the specific locations on the body

As a way of saying thank you for your purchase, I'm offering a free gift that's exclusive to readers of this book.

GO TO THE LINK TO ACCESS

http://dublbmarketing.com/blog/eftlp

Chapter One: What are EFT Points?

There are some points in our body that hold vortex of energy. We humans are capable of possibilities and power that most of us cannot even imagine.

Let the journey start; "Let the tournament begin!" Let us explore the points that hold the energy, peace and other necessary feelings that help us live, live happily and live long.

Point no 1. The first point is at the side of our hand, as you see in the images below. They are on both hands; they are called set up points. We start from here and confess or talk about what our problem is. It should be a very gentle tapping; we are going to repeat this taping around 20-30 times on both hands. It is an energy centre. When we tap on these two set up points, they release the energy they hold.

Point of another hand

Point no 2. Our second point is on the top of our head. We tap on that this point and pacify our anxiety with loving words. This releases peace in our whole body. We feel loved.

Point no 3. The next point is the inner eye brow. Rub your fingers on this point gently and ask for more peace. This widens your mind.

Point no 4. The next point is the side of the eyes, on the bone. Tap on these points gently and inspire faith that everything will be alright, as it always had been.

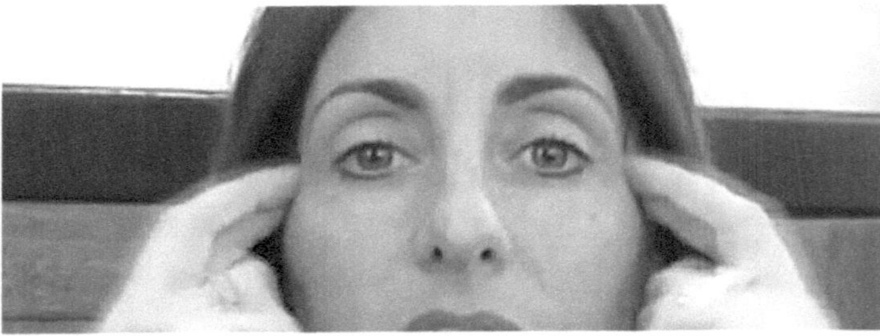

Point no 5. The next point is under the eyes, on the bone. Tap on these points and you will feel like a child being caressed by your loving elders.

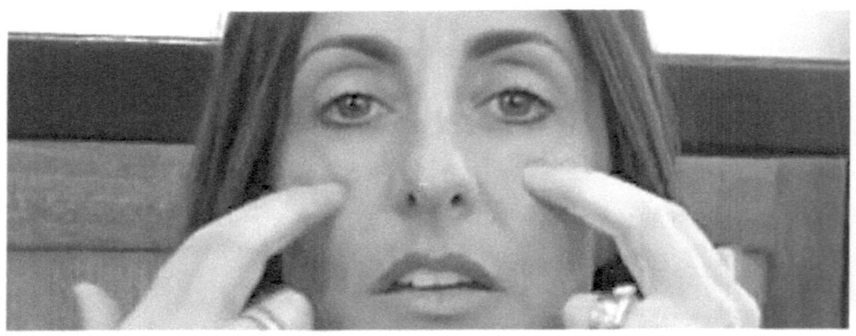

Point no 6. The next point is under the nose. When you tap on this point, you have a feeling that you are really free of many things.

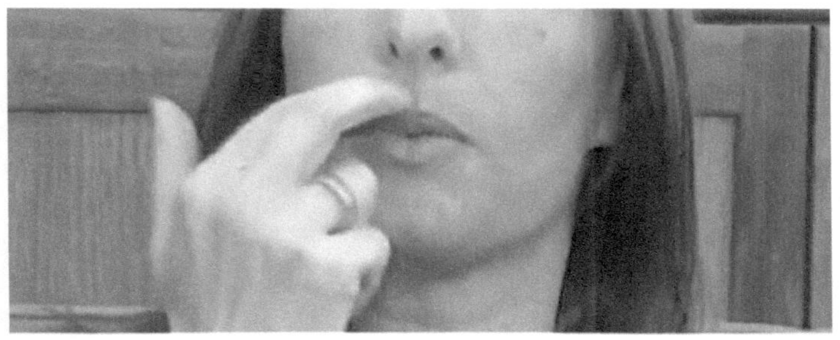

Point no 7. Next to it is the point under the chin. Tap on this point and say that I will make it. It doesn't matter at all.

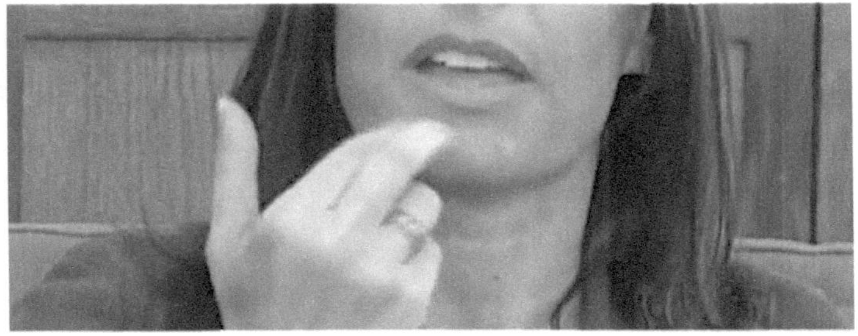

Point no 8. The next point is underneath the collarbone point, on both sides. Now come to a belief that you are human and capable of infinite possibilities. You love yourself, and you have lived long. You are bold, honest with yourself. You feel live and warm.

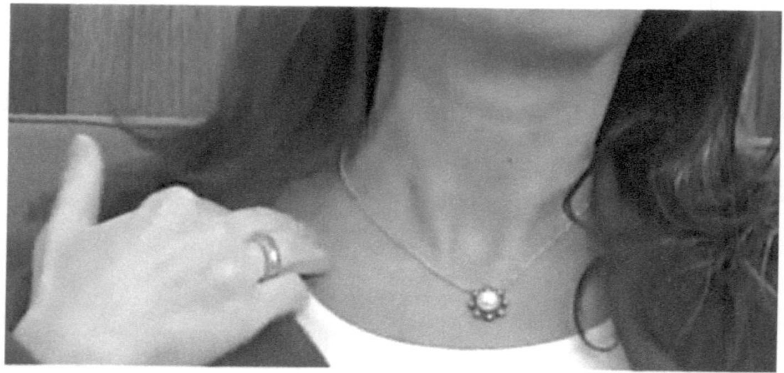

Point no 9. The next point is under the arm, on both sides. Tap on them, one by one or on both sides together. You feel a lift. There's a feeling that you have made it. See how relaxed you feel when you tap these points!

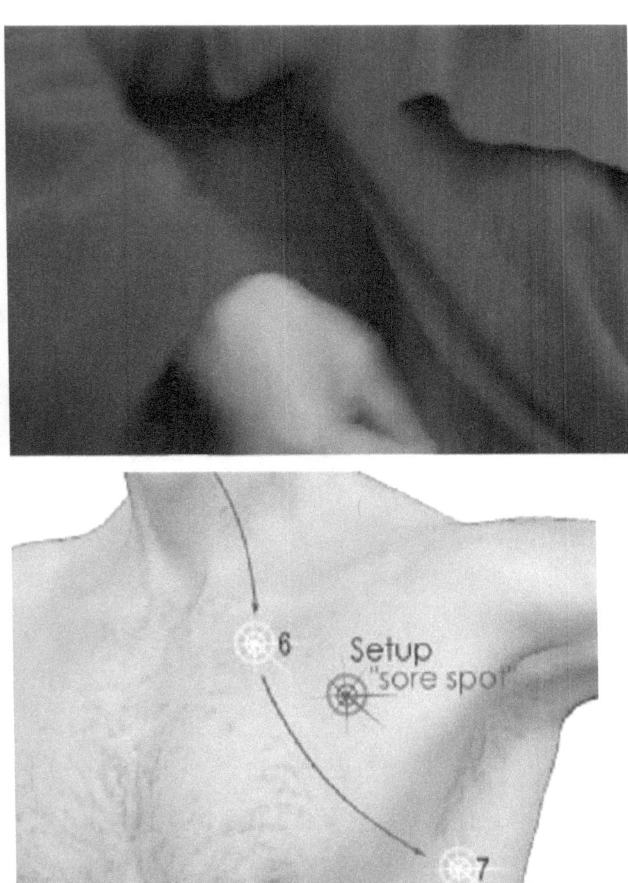
6
Setup
"sore spot"
7

Point no 10. And the last points are the inside of the both of our wrists. Tap them together, like you have won the game. You have made it. You are free from your anxiety.

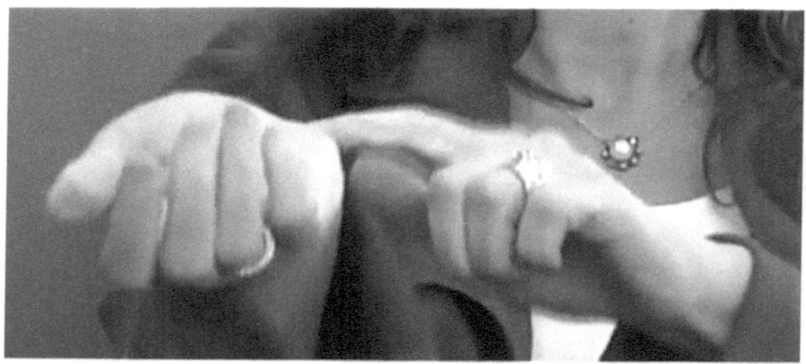

Point no 0. All the tips of your fingers are energy points. Every point you tap, you tap your finger tips too. They, in contact with other points, ask the body to release energy.

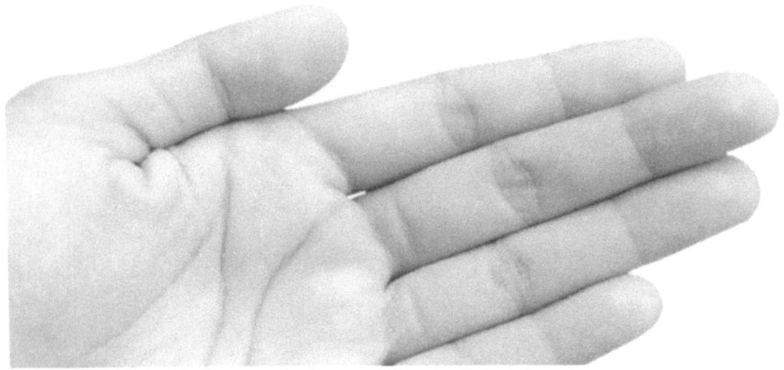

A Short Message From The Author

Hey, are you enjoying the book? I'd love to hear your thoughts!

Many readers do not know how hard reviews are to come by, and how
much they help an author.

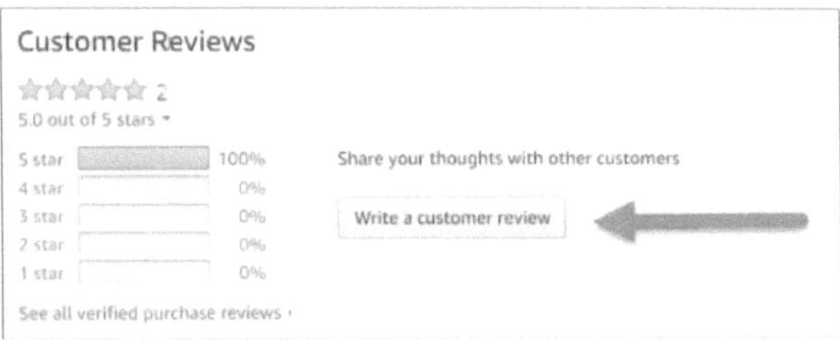

I would be incredibly thankful if you could take just 60 seconds to write a
brief review on Amazon, even if it's just a few sentences!

>> Click here to leave a quick review

Thank you for taking the time to share your thoughts!

Your review will genuinely make a difference for me and help gain
exposure for my work.

52

Chapter Two: What do the Psychiatrists say?

There are several sites and videos where many of the world's renowned psychiatrists say how they are helping thousands of people suffering from emotional stresses. And there are people who have expressed their gratitude for these techniques and the technicians, for they are living stress free life more or less.

EFT will give you

- Release from negative emotions
- Release from of Food Cravings
- Release from Pain
- Inspiration of Better Future

These points are not something discovered by the modern doctors of psychiatrist; they are as old as the rocks. They are derived from acupuncture, and a part of acupressure.

The simplest possible way of living free of emotional stresses or mental pressures is to take things simply. Not that our life is simple; sometimes it is too complicated. But the technique is to take it simply rather than taking it in a complicated way and going astray.

Repeat the tapping from the first point to the last point in a harmony. Take as much time as you need to know that you really have nothing to worry about. Everything will be fine in time.

A round of rhythmical tapping and believing may cure you from the points written above. If the tapping one round fails to cure it 100%, just try another round and you will be OK.

Chapter Three: How to Switch on the IPS Switches.

Every day, every hour, every minute some people commits suicide. Why?

An emotional barrier may hamper you a lot. It stops the rhythms of your life and you may even feel morbid sometimes. This is really bad; hinders the advancement of your life and may even be a cause of a total destruction of your life. We are no longer going to tolerate those feelings that are causing us pain and will be causing pain eternally if they are not overcome or eradicated from our life.

The tapping of these points make your body release a vortex of energy that you do not usually feel. **The best way** is to get tapped by another person who is acquainted with these points. He/she needs not to be an expert; almost anybody can do the taping. But the point is- an expert knows the world you need to hear. So, for the best possible release from your emotional pressures, you should meet someone whom you would tell your mind and who, with loving words, will help your body release the energy it always holds.

Nothing has ever happened in your life that has destroyed your whole existence. Life seems tough, but it is beautiful. All that you need is to love yourself. Love yourself and feel what you feel- I want to live; I will live; nothing can stop me if I want to live.

Now laugh like this child and see the world.

1 billion Cheers for your stress free life!!!!!!!!!!!

A Short Message From The Author

Reviews are not easy to come by.

As an independent author with a tiny marketing budget, I rely on readers,
like you, to leave a short review on Amazon.

Even if it's just a sentence or two!

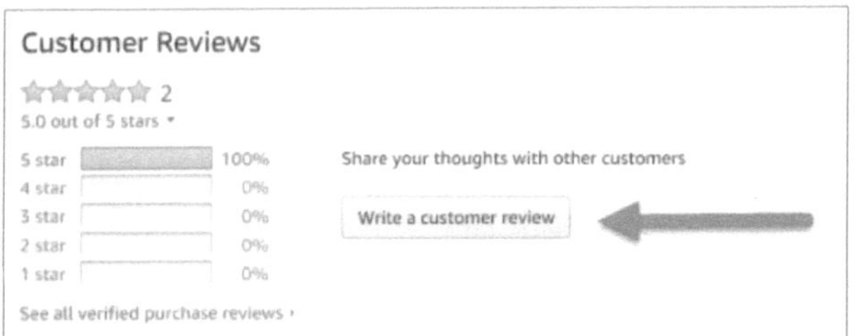

I would be incredibly thankful if you could take just 60 seconds to write a
brief review on Amazon, even if it's just a few sentences!

>> Click here to leave a quick review

Thank you for taking the time to share your thoughts!

Your review will genuinely make a difference for me and help gain
exposure for my work.

Something of Value

Our team wants to take the time and say thank you for enjoying the material that was placed in this book. In addition, one of our missions is to always leave our readers with something of value on top of the content within the book. The best thing that we can offer is to change and impact your life! Because there are so many different types of readers from different walks of life there is only one type of program that we know without a shadow of doubt that can change and impact one's life. That would be the "Magic Of Your Mind" program.

The reason this program beats everything else that we have researched is simply because the people and the material behind it. The people who put the content together studied directly with the personal development greats such as Napoleon Hill, Buckminster Fuller, Earl Nightingale, Jim Rohn, Zig Zigler, and if you don't know any of those names it doesn't matter. All that matters is that you are given the opportunity to change your life for the better and the "Magic Of Your Mind" program offers that opportunity.

IN JUST Six Weeks YOU'LL DISCOVER HOW TO:

- Move beyond mere mental activity to real thinking.
- Originate thoughts that vibrate in harmony with who you want to be, do and have.
- Consciously use your imagination to purposely bring your goals to life and create a life that looks exactly the way you want it to look.
- Project forward and create memories of a future event that is beyond the point where your wish has come true.
- Transform any challenge by changing your perception of the situation.
- Transform your hopes and wishes for what you MIGHT into expectations of what you WILL have.
- And much more!

To take advantage of the program and change your life, rather it is pertaining to finances, relationships, health, mindset, spirituality, or any other category just follow these steps. If you have the physical book go to the link below or if you have the audiobook, go to the link that is mentioned and you will receive more information.

62

http://dublbmarketing.com/blog/magic-in-your-mind-review

References

Free Gifts

http://dublbmarketing.com/blog/how-to-get-anything-you-want-ebook

http://dublbmarketing.com/blog/eftlp

Other Books Worth Mentioning

http://dublbmarketing.com/blog/ebook-list

Something of Value Offer

http://dublbmarketing.com/blog/magic-in-your-mind-review

Your Free Gift

THE SCIENCE OF GETTING RICH SECRETS

GIFT: Receive a step-by-step training seminar from a top philosopher to master achieving whatever YOU WANT *FREE* ($5,000+ value)

In the guide you will learn how to master your emotions like <u>PRO's</u> and rise to the top on any and all GOALS!

Here is what is discussed...

4. The natural laws of the universe discussed in depth
5. How the natural laws can work in your favor
6. The different types of money and which kind is best to earn

As a way of saying thank you for your purchase, I'm offering a free gift that's exclusive to readers of this book.

GO TO THE LINK TO ACCESS

http://dublbmarketing.com/blog/how-to-get-anythin g-you-want-ebook